FOURTH
ASSESSMENT PA
ENGLISH

JM BOND

Nelson

Underline the right answers.

"Inspector, please tell me about beachcombers – your voluntary helpers. Are more needed, and how do they set about being taken on?"

With a friendly grin he replied, "Of course more are needed. In the first three months of this year our counters, or beachcombers, reported 20 000 dead birds, a large number of which were the victims of pollution. This was one of the worst periods in the history of oil pollution in Britain, and make no mistake, it can happen again. So, yes, we want more helpers. All young people interested in this work should contact their local R.S.P.C.A. inspectors just as soon as they hear of an oil disaster. That is the emergency help we need. As to regular voluntary work, contact the Royal Society for the Protection of Birds and ask to help with their beached bird survey around the coast of Britain."

1 A volunteer is (a soldier, a bird watcher, a person who works without being paid)

2 The counters are (people who count birds, rings on birds, shells, a kind of bird)

3–5 In which months did 20 000 birds die? (January, February, March, April, May, June, July, August, September, October, November, December)

6 R.S.P.C.A. stands for (Royal Society for the Prevention of Cruelty to Birds, Royal Society for the Prevention of Cruelty to Animals)

7 The oil has come from (oil wells which have overflowed, oil tankers that have been damaged at sea, factories discharging oil into rivers)

8 Beachcombers are (people who live on the beach, people who search for things on the beach, campers)

9 "Make no mistake" means (you can be sure, the account is wrong, you must not make a mistake)

10-11   In which ways can you help? (By contacting the police, by reporting oil slicks, by counting beached birds, by controlling pollution)

12   You can help if you (live in the country, live on the coast, live inland, live on a boat)

Use the past tense of the word on the left to complete each sentence.

13   begin   She .... to sing the song.

14   eat   My brothers .... all the sweets.

15   ride   The jockey .... to victory.

16   shake   Pauline and Jo .... their heads as they danced.

17   ring   When the bell ...., all the children streamed out of the school doors.

18   strike   The clock .... midnight.

Give the opposite meaning of the following words.

19   expand   20   inferior   ....

21   guilty   22   mad   ....

23   question   24   divide   ....

Underline the subject of each sentence, and put a ring round the verb(s).

25-26   My dog likes long walks.

27-28   The beautiful flowers grew in the wood.

29-31   When she went into the playground the girl wore trainers.

Insert the missing word on each line.

32   Teacher is to pupil as doctor is to ....

33   Buyer is to seller as .... is to shopkeeper.

Write the plural of the following words.

34   handkerchief   35   dwarf   ....

36   passer-by   37   cupful   ....

38   sheep   39   echo   ....

40   daughter-in-law   ....

3

Complete the following table.

	young	mother	father
41–42	....	hen	....
43–44	....	goose	....
45–46	puppy	....	....
47–48	....	mare	....
49–50	....	....	ram

In the spaces write adjectives made from the words on the left.

51 health   You need good food, exercise and sleep to be ....

52 marvel   The fireworks were a .... sight.

53 circle   The .... saw was used for cutting logs.

54 poison   The boy, who ate a .... berry, was very ill.

55 nature   The girl's make-up had a very .... look.

56 caution   He acted in a very .... way.

One word on each line has a different meaning from the other four words. Underline that word.

57 amusement   entertainment   pastime   cinema   sport

58 raise   height   lift   elevate   hoist

59 hide   reveal   tell   divulge   disclose

60 intelligence   wisdom   bright   comprehension   understanding

61 suspense   story   doubt   hesitation   uncertainty

62 outset   beginning   end   opening   commencement

Choose a phrase from the list on the right to fill each space.

63 An architect uses   ....   a camera

64 A conductor uses   ....   scissors

65 A photographer uses   ....   a hammer

66 An auctioneer uses   ....   a baton

67 A chemist uses   ....   plans

68 A hairdresser uses   ....   prescriptions

69-72 Read the poem below and then draw a line under any of the statements about it which are correct.

Fog in November, trees have no heads,
Streams only sound, walls suddenly stop
Half way up hills, the ghost of a man spreads
Dung on dead fields for next year's crop.
I cannot see my hand before my face,
My body does not seem to be my own,
The world becomes a far-off, foreign place,
People are strangers, houses silent, unknown

L. Clark

The trees have been felled.

They have knocked down the walls.

The man can't be seen clearly.

The stream has dried up.

One can see only a little way ahead.

Places look different in the fog.

The farmer is sowing seed.

You can't see the stream.

There are a lot of strangers about.

In each space write one word which has the same meaning as the words in heavy type.

73	The twins were **exactly the same** in all ways.	....
74	The concert was **put off** until next week.	....
75	She **made up her mind** to make a cake.	....
76	The army **went forward** to attack.	....
77	They had a party **once a year**.	....
78	As most of the team were ill, the match was **called off**.	....
79	Spoons, knives and forks are called	....
80	Zinc, copper and tin are	....
81	Cars, buses and lorries are	....
82	Ants, earwigs and moths are	....
83	Venus, Mercury and Earth are	....

5

Use these words to complete the sentences below.

infrequent　　inexpensive　　incomplete　　inaudible　　inconsiderate

84　The lady was surprised that the coat was so ....

85　There should have been twenty copies of the textbook but the teacher could find only sixteen. The set was ....

86　The girl mumbled her reply. She was ....

87　There were only two buses each day. The service was ....

88　The girl didn't care how much work she made for other people. She was ....

Write the words which rhyme with the given word and start with the given letter.

89–90　nose

　　t ....

　　d ....

91–92　verse

　　w ....

　　c ....

93–100　Several words have been left out of this passage. Can you fill them in?

Maria was only eleven, ... she was already

thinking .... what she would do .... she left school.

Her mother suggested .... as she liked flying she might become

an .... hostess and .... the world, but Maria

thought .... would rather be a vet, as .... main interest

was in animals.

Underline the right answers.

It did not happen until the fourth day of the summer holidays, and then only by a mere fluke, for if the bright new golden penny had come down tails up they would have helped Father to fish instead of exploring by themselves.

"Tails, fish; heads, explore," Keith had said as he tossed for it ... and it was heads.

At first there were complaints from the other four, for it was great fun helping Father to fish; for the children, that is. Father was not overkeen on the assistance of his offspring; but Keith put an instant stop to these iniquitous murmurings.

"Shut up!" he said. "It's disrespectful to the gods not to abide by the toss."

"Why?" demanded Elspeth.

"Because you have challenged them. You have said, 'Speak, oh ye gods! If it is your will that we should help Father fish then show us the flicker of a sparkling tail upon the dust, but if it is your will that we should seek adventure on the high road then show us the outline of a king's head set in gold!'"

"Pick up our penny anyhow," said Elspeth. "It is our only one ... You pick it up, Flora-Dora."

The fat little twins slid solidly off the wall, picked up the penny, returned it to Elspeth, and climbed heavily back to their seats.

From *A Crock of Gold* by Elizabeth Goudge

1 A "fluke" is a (toss, flake, lucky chance, golden penny)

2 How did the children want the coin to spin? (I don't know, heads up, tails up)

3 How did it land? (I don't know, heads up, tails up)

4 How many children were there? (1, 2, 3, 4, 5, 6)

5 Did Father want the children's help? (I don't know, no, yes)

6 "Offspring" are (animals that jump, children, divers)

7 "Iniquitous" means (can't be heard, unequal, wicked)

8 A challenge is (asking them to settle a problem, teasing them, telling them to speak)

9–10 Name the twins. (Keith, Flora, Dora, Elspeth)

11 "Slid solidly" means (slid heavily, slid quietly, slid noisily)

12 Do you think the twins could move quickly? (No, yes, I don't know)

13 Who was the leader of the children? (Keith, Elspeth, Flora, Dora)

Reduce each sentence by writing the subject and the object as pronouns.

14–15 Bill hit the ball.   16–17 The young girl cut her knee.

.... hit .... ·   .... cut ....

18–19 All the children in the school help the old lady.

.... help ....

Look at the idioms on the left of the page, and then at the list of their meanings on the right of the page. Write beside each idiom the number which indicates its correct meaning.

20 To turn over a new leaf ......( )......   (1) to be exhausted

21 To smell a rat ......( )......   (2) to crawl

22 To get into hot water ......( )......   (3) to do much better

23 To go on all fours ......( )......   (4) to be depressed

24 To be dead beat ......( )......   (5) to be suspicious

25 To be down in the mouth ......( )......   (6) to be in trouble

Insert the commas, inverted commas and capital letters in these sentences.

26–27 The prisoner asked why should I have to stay here?

....

28–29 Mum said you won't go out until you have done your homework.

....

Write in the space provided the adverb which best describes each of the verbs in the list on the left.

30 talked .... ravenously

31 watched .... stealthily

32 ate .... hilariously

33 laughed .... carefully

34 crept .... intently

35 copied .... fluently

In each space write a suitable preposition.

36 We shared the conkers .... the children.

37 I forgot I had to post a letter, and walked straight .... the Post Office.

38 We have breakfast .... school.

39 Tea .... sugar is not sweet.

40 Chalk is very different .... cheese.

41 Put the star .... the top of the tree.

Write the name of a colour in each space.

42 I was .... with envy when I saw his lovely bicycle.

43 We never use the clock, so it is a .... elephant.

44–45 I read it in the newspaper, so I saw it in .... and ....

46 It was my birthday, so it was a ....-letter day.

Write the name of the person who "fits" the noun.
Example: Italy Italian

47 song ....

48 assistance ....

49 deceit ....

50 favour ....

51 politics ....

52 law ....

Fill in the names of the sounds made by the following:

53 The .... of frogs

54 The .... of a clock

55 The .... of the wind

56 The .... of leaves

57 The .... of water

58 The .... of hooves

In each space, write a word which begins with a silent **w**.

59 Dad .... out the water from the washing.

60 She knew she did .... to steal the money from the coat pocket.

61 Nicola sprained her .... when she did a handstand.

62 The miserable .... had been in prison for years.

63 The worms were .... along the path.

64-66 In the spaces write **they're, there** or **their**.

.... goes .... cat which .... giving away.

67-70 In the spaces write **to, too** or **two**.

.... many of them went .... far. They got ....
the bridge which was .... miles away.

71-73 In the spaces write **were** or **where**.

.... are the books? .... they .... we left them?

74-80 Write these words again, in alphabetical order:

procure   (1) ....

product   (2) ....

probe   (3) ....

produce   (4) ....

process   (5) ....

proceed   (6) ....

Fill in the missing prepositions.

80 My hairstyle is different .... yours.

81 The man in the dock was guilty .... murder.

82 According .... his letter, he should be here soon.

83 I disagree .... you about that.

Every sixth word has been left out of the passage below. Try to fill them in.

84–89 Have you noticed how hills .... often covered by clouds? Even .... weather forecast mentions it.
"It .... be fine with occasional showers. .... will be early morning hill .... but by mid-day this will ....

From the verbs listed on the left form nouns ending in **ion**.
Example: evade evasion

90 divide ....   91 produce ....

92 dictate ....   93 create ....

94 invade ....   95 resolve ....

Can you think of a simple word which means the same as the word on the left?

96 explosion ....   97 velocity ....

98 indolent ....   99 victory ....

100 abundance ....

Paper 3

Underline the right answers.

The world below the brine,
Forests at the bottom of the sea, the branches
        and leaves,
Sea lettuce, vast lichens, strange flowers and seeds,
        the thick tangle, openings, and pink turf,
Different colours, pale grey and green, purple, white,
        and gold, the play of light through the water,
Dumb swimmers there among the rocks, coral,
        gluten, grass, rushes, and the aliment of swimmers,
Sluggish existences grazing there suspended, or
        slowly crawling close to the bottom,
The sperm whale at the surface blowing air and
        spray, or disporting with his flukes,
The leaden-eyed shark, the walrus, the turtle, the
        hairy sea-leopard, and the sting-ray,
Passions there, wars, pursuits, tribes, sight in those
        ocean-depths, breathing that thick-breathing
        air, as so many do,
The change thence to the sight here, and to the subtle
        air breathed by beings like us who walk this sphere,
The change onward from ours to that of beings who
        walk other spheres.

The World below the Brine by Walt Whitman

1   The poem is about (the world beyond the brink,
    the world below the sea, tropical forests, outer space)

2   "Brine" is (a bridge, fresh water, a kind of fish, salt water)

3   How many dumb swimmers are mentioned?
    (One, two, three, four, five, six, seven, eight)

4   "Aliment" is (sickness, spray, food, drink)

5   Which two words describe creatures which hang motionless or move
    slowly? (Sluggish existences, sperm whale, dumb swimmers)

12

6 Which of the creatures had a sense of humour?
(The sperm whale, the walrus, the turtle)

7 Which word means "moving with gaiety"? (Crawling, disporting, grazing)

8 "Flukes" are (mistakes, the whale's tail, a lucky chance, the whale's ears)

9 "Pursuits" are (changes, people, purposes, occupations)

10 "Beings who walk other spheres" refers to
(whales, humans, creatures in another world)

Complete the following proverbs.

11 There is no smoke without ....

12 A miss is as good as a ....

13 Every cloud has a silver ....

14 First come, first ....

15 More haste, less ....

16 One .... doesn't make a summer.

17–22 Underline any word which applies to male and female alike.

girl   friend   uncle   niece   vixen   companion

secretary   giant   orphan   aunt   guest   cousin

Complete the following sentences by forming nouns from the words on the left.

23 advertise   She saw the .... on television.

24 depart   The .... of the train was delayed.

25 fly   The " .... of the Bumble Bee" is a popular piece of music.

26 real   In .... they are quite ordinary people.

27 applaud   The .... lasted for several minutes.

28 anxious   Their .... about their mother was understandable.

Change the following from direct to indirect speech.

29 Tom said, "I'll do my homework now."

Tom said that ....

30 Mum said, "I shall have to change my plans."

Mum said that ....

31 Dad said, "I can play cricket this evening."

Dad said that ....

32 Tony said, "Would you like to play soccer with me, Tim?"

Tony asked Tim ....

Give the opposite meaning of the following words by using a prefix.
Example: safe unsafe

33 correct   ....   34 aware   ....

35 selfish   ....   36 respect   ....

37 possible   ....   38 obedient   ....

39 connect   ....   40 trust   ....

One word in each line is incorrect. Underline that word, and in the space
write what the word should be.

41 Of the two Jill is the nicest.   ....

42 I would of thought he could do better.   ....

43 I cannot do no more work.   ....

44 Karen and her sister is very tall.   ....

45 None of the books were in good condition.   ....

Write the plural of the following words.

46 kangaroo   ....   47 atlas   ....

48 deer   ....   49 gulf   ....

50 mosquito   ....   51 woman   ....

52 ox   ....   53 chief   ....

Complete each sentence with one of these words.

antique   conceited   obedient
confidential   convenient   extravagant

54 The rich woman was very wasteful. She was ....

55 The letter was private. It was ....

56 The girl thought that she was very beautiful. She was ....

57 The table was two hundred years old. It was an ....

58 The girl did as she was told. She was ....

59 The bus stopped outside the school. It was very ....

Write two words which rhyme with each word in capitals, and begin with the given letter.

60–61 WORK   62–63 ROAM   64–65 STOLE

l ....   c ....   b ....

j ....   d ....   sh ....

Below are the names of ten containers, and on the right is a list of what those containers usually hold. Match them, and write the number in the space.

66 vase ...( )...   67 jar ...( )...   fruit (1)   jam (6)

68 decanter ...( )...   69 packet ...( )...   wine (2)   coal (7)

70 scuttle ...( )...   71 bottle ...( )...   money (3)   milk (8)

72 carton ...( )...   73 kettle ...( )...   cigarettes (4) flowers (9)

74 punnet ...( )...   75 till ...( )...   water (5)   cream (10)

Give the opposites of the following words by altering the suffixes.
Example: hopeful   hopeless

76 careful   ....   77 hairless   ....

78 noisy   ....   79 useful   ....

80 painless   ....   81 lawless   ....

Write a one-word definition for each of these words.

82 lubricate   ....   83 enigma   ....

84 minimum   ....   85 abbreviate ....

86 summit   ....

15

87–93 Every sixth word has been omitted from the passage below. Can you fill them in?

Many years ago, people used .... light fires on mid-summer's

eve .... the following day the sun .... be

at its highest point .... the sky. They thought by ....

this the sun would not .... away but would be encouraged

.... stay longer and warm the earth.

Mayoring Day at Rye
This beautiful town used to be an important port, but it is now inland. At one time it had the privilege of minting its own coins, and this occasion is a reminder of those times. At noon on this day the Mayor goes out on to a balcony and throws hot pennies to the waiting crowd. As you can imagine, it's the children who manage to pocket most of the money.

94–96 Underline the statements which are correct.

Rye is an important port.

Fake coins were once made in Rye.

Rye is not on the coast now.

Mayoring Day reminds people that Rye was once a port.

The children get most of the money thrown to the crowd.

Mayoring Day commemorates the time when Rye had a mint.

Write the name of the person derived from each of these words.

97 science	....	**98** study	....
99 music	....	**100** criticism	....

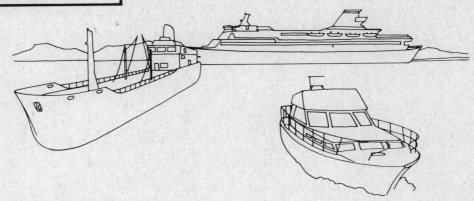

Underline the right answers.

I travelled to South America on a cargo boat which took a whole month to reach Buenos Aires. Before I set sail I was sure I had in me more of the pioneering spirit than even Columbus himself, but I soon decided that riding the waves was not one of my strong points, for the smell of the engines in our small ship and the constant vibration turned my stomach, and I experienced none of the joys of the cruel sea. In fact I was horribly ill for almost the entire journey, although I was just able to emerge at the end of it to enjoy the unbelievable beauties of Rio with its mountains behind, the gigantic blue butterflies, and the blue and white foam of the enormous breakers on its honey coloured sand.

From *Talking to Animals* by Barbara Woodhouse

1 Before the journey she was (full of fears, looking forward to adventures, feeling bored)

2 "Riding the waves" means (she is good with horses, she pretended she was riding, sailing on a rough sea)

3–4 What made her feel ill? (The boat rocked a lot, she was uncomfortable, she was tired, engine fumes)

5 "Turned her stomach" means (she had to face the other way, made her feel sick, she didn't like the food)

6 A pioneer is (a soldier, an explorer, a sailor, a performer)

7 Which town did she think was beautiful? (Rio, Buenos Aires, Columbia)

8 A cargo boat usually carries (passengers, cars, goods)

9 "Breakers" are (vandals, high mountains, waves, beaches)

10 "To emerge" is to (come out, recover, enjoy, join together)

11–12 At the end of the journey do you think she (was glad she had gone on a small boat, was surprised that she was a bad sailor, was looking forward to visiting Rio, was looking forward to the journey home)?

Fill in the spaces by writing the past tense of the word on the left.

13 leave   They .... the baby in his push-chair.

14 go   The boys .... on the ghost train.

15 ring   They .... the bells for the wedding ceremony.

16 catch   Poor Sarah had .... German measles.

17 bring   The children .... their lunch to school.

18 forget   They were in a hurry, and .... to post the letters.

19 teach   The teacher .... the infants how to play the game.

20 think   They .... it was a very good idea.

Write one word in each space to complete the following expressions.

21 slow but ....   22 rough and ....

23 fast and ....   24 part and ....

25 facts and ....   26 rank and ....

27 might and ....   28 give and ....

29 fits and ....   30 high and ....

Complete the following:
Example: Apples from England are English apples.

31 Figs from China are .... figs.

32 Wool from Australia is .... wool.

33 Tea from India is .... tea.

34 Cars from Japan are .... cars.

35 A boat from Norway is a .... boat

36–47 The following passage does not make sense because the full stops, and some of the capital letters have been misplaced. Alter these to make sense.

It was a beautiful summer day. In the country the corn was golden and the hay was stacked. In the meadow an old mansion, surrounded by a moat, and a wall stood bathed in the bright sunshine in a quiet spot. Beside the moat a mother duck sat on her nest Waiting for her eggs to hatch.

Rewrite each of the following using two words only.
Example: basket for a cat   cat's basket

48	school for girls	....
49	hospital for women	....
50	canteen for the workers	....
51	playground for children	....
52	ward reserved for men	....

53–56 One word in each column is spelled wrongly. Underline that word.

ostrich	special	moisture	transparant
contrary	favourite	education	peculiar
interrupt	sucess	government	gigantic
pedestrian	indignant	critic	meagre
visable	Wednesday	mischief	necessary
separate	resident	persuade	abundant
behaviour	obedience	interfere	coarse
encourage	applaud	discribe	difficult

Put apostrophes in the correct places.

57 The children were pulling the cats tail.

58 The childrens coats were hanging in the cloakroom.

59 The mens coats were reduced in the sale.

60 The girls names were written in the register.

Underline the word which is the same part of speech as the word on the left.

61 **move**   leg   finger   walk   soft   me

62 **across**   jump   before   river   bridge   wood

63 **your**   her   friend   near   and   boy

64 **because** reason safe   hard   and   list

65 **I**   author person   he   am   boy

66 **friendly** girl   smart   foe   patiently friend

67 **cup**   pour   hot   pen   large   the

Complete the following sentences by using words from the list.

permit omit halt retire leave allowance exit cancel

68 The .... is behind the stage.

69 The soldier was given ten days' ....

70 I will .... the order unless you can get the goods quickly.

71 We were told we could .... one question.

72 The headmaster was going to .... at the end of term.

73 They were told to .... when the leaders reached the top.

74 The .... to visit the country arrived today.

75 The widow received her weekly ....

Fill each space with a suitable preposition.

between   among   beside   along   past

76 He walked .... the house where she lived.

77 Mum asked Diana to sit .... her.

78 The boy ran .... the path to the boathouse.

79 Share the sweets .... the class.

80 Ian can sit .... David and Martin.

81–88 Turn these nouns into adjectives by adding a suffix. Put them in columns of those that end in **ish** and that that end in **ful**.

sheep   beauty   hope   fever   grace   fool   child   cheer

     ish   ful

....

....

....

....

Underline the correct alternative to complete the sentences.

89 Haven't you (any/no) shoes my size?

90 There are (any/no) shoes your size.

91 There is (anything/nothing) left.

92 We haven't (anything/nothing) left.

93 There were (any/none) of the books I wanted.

94 They didn't have (any/none) of the books I wanted.

95 Isn't there (anyone/no one) here to help?

96 There is (anyone/no one) here to help.

97–100 Can you put these words into alphabetical order ?

mantelpiece   manage   manager   Managua

(1) ....

(2) ....

(3) ....

(4) ....

Underline the right answers.

All this went on for what seemed to the hobbit ages upon ages; and he was always hungry, for they were extremely careful with their provisions. Even so, as days followed days, and still the forest seemed just the same, they began to get anxious. The food would not last for ever: it was in fact already beginning to get low. They tried shooting at the squirrels, and they wasted many arrows before they managed to bring one down on the path. But when they roasted it, it proved horrible to taste, and they shot no more squirrels.

They were thirsty too, for they had none too much water, and in all the time they had seen neither spring nor stream. This was their state when one day they found their path blocked by running water. It flowed fast and strong but not very wide right across the way, and it was black, or looked it in the gloom. It was well that Beorn had warned them against it, or they would have drunk from it, whatever its colour, and filled some of their emptied skins at its banks. As it was they only thought of how to cross it without wetting themselves in the water.

From *The Hobbit* by J. R. R. Tolkien

1   Their provisions were (guarded carefully, used sparingly, not eaten at all)

2   "Days followed days" means (it was constant daylight, they did not notice the nights, in the course of several days)

3   "Ages upon ages" means (an everlasting time, it was a very long time, they added their ages together)

4   They were anxious because (their food was short, they couldn't shoot squirrels, the days were so long)

5   They felt thirsty because (they had too much water, they did not have enough water, they didn't like drinking)

6   They carried water (in bottles, in skins, in glasses)

22

7–9 The stream was (sluggish, fast-running, dirty, wide, narrow)

10 They didn't live on squirrels because (they were hard to shoot, they couldn't roast them, they didn't like their taste)

11 They did not drink the water because (it was dirty, they had been told not to drink it, it was flowing too quickly)

12 What was their chief wish when they saw the stream? (To cross the stream, to get food, to have a drink, to get home)

Write the number of the appropriate phrase in each space.

13 I keep all my .....( )..... in that drawer.　　　　(1) lock and key

14 She had been ill but now she was .....( ).....　　　(2) odds and ends

15 The men started to argue, and soon there was　　(3) far and away
a .....( ).....　　　　　　　　　　　　　　　　　　　(4) out and about

16 We cleaned our room and it looked .....( ).....　　(5) rough and tumble

17 They kept their valuables under .....( ).....　　　　(6) spick and span

18 The film was .....( )..... the best we have seen.

Underline the word on each line which has a different meaning from the others.

19 tedious　　tiring　　wearisome　　tearful　　wearing

20 necessary　established　essential　indispensable　unavoidable

21 avail　avoid　elude　escape　evade

22 accurate　correct　exact　right　mark

23 expel　refund　discharge　banish　eject

24 choice　option　preference　essence　alternative

25–28 Put these words into alphabetical order.
excellent　exact　extra　extract

(1) ....　(2) ....　(3) ....　(4) ....

Turn the words in heavy type into the feminine form.

29–30 My **son** .... showed the book to my **nephew** ....

31–32 The **headmaster** .... interviewed the two **men** ....

33–34 The **Prince** .... presented the medal to the **hero** ....

Put the following into direct speech.

35 Tim said that he didn't want to go to bed.

Tim said, ...

36 Mum said that she wished Gary would wash his hands.

Mum said to Gary, ...

37 Tracy asked Sue if she might borrow her rubber.

Tracy said to Sue, ...

38 Pauline said that she would give Andy the book.

Pauline said to Andy, ...

Give the plural of the following words.

39 storey ....   40 melody ....

41 journey ....   42 alley ....

43 ally ....   44 butterfly ....

Use a form of the word on the left to put each sentence into the past tense.

45 bring   The farmer .... in the eggs.

46 fly   The bird .... round the cage.

47 steal   The boys .... the sweets from the shop.

48 take   Richard .... the book off the shelf.

49 drink   The cat .... all the milk in its saucer.

Underline the correct word in the brackets.

50 The doctor's (practise, practice) is in Warwick Road.

51 They (practise, practice) their Judo.

52 The (principal, principle) of the college had taught abroad.

53 It was a matter of (principal, principle) that he wrote the letter.

54 Where is (their, there) breakfast?

55 I put it over (their, there).

56 The (coarse, course) of the river meanders through the field.

57 The material she used was very (coarse, course).

Underline the word which is the same part of speech as the word on the left.

58 **roared**   lion   gave   fiercely   animals   noise

59 **severely**   lazily   stern   teacher   he   cross

60 **fatal**   die   method   fatality   heroic   fatally

61 **oddly**   do   luck   odd   oddity   luckily

62 **advice**   angry   advise   anger   easy   read

63 **forgetful**   enjoy   justify   helpfully   pleasant   remember

Here are some words and, on the right of the page, a list of their meanings. Write the correct number in the space.

64   biped   ....( )....   (1) happening every two hundred years

65   biceps   ....( )....   (2) a two-legged animal

66   bicentenary   ....( )....   (3) muscles

67   bigamy   ....( )....   (4) the life history of a person

68   bilingual   ....( )....   (5) the custom of having two wives

69   biography   ....( )....   (6) having a knowledge of two languages.

Which are the following? If a statement, write S, write Q for a question, and C for a command

70   The United Kingdom has an equable climate   ....

71   Bring me the scissors   ....

72   Did you put it on the table   ....

73   What is the answer   ....

74   Deciduous trees lose their leaves in winter   ....

75   Are evergreen trees always green   ....

76   Put on your shoes   ....

77   The dog barked loudly   ....

Fill in the spaces.
Example: drink   drinker

78   sale   79   deed   ....

80   loss   81   defence   ....

82   seat   83   burglary   ....

84   custom   ....

I can get through a doorway without any key,
And strip the leaves from the great oak tree.
I can drive storm clouds and shake tall towers,
Or steal through a garden and not wake the flowers.
Seas I can move and ships I can sink.
I can carry a house-top or the scent of a pink.
When I am angry I can rave and riot,
And when I am spent I lie as quiet as quiet.

James Reeves

85 What am I? (Rain, lightning, wind, thunder)

86 "Not wake flowers" means
(not call them, not pull them up, not disturb them)

87 A pink is (a colour, a measure, a flower)

88 "Quiet as quiet" means (very quiet, as quiet as you are, not very quiet)

89 "I am spent" means (I have no money, I have got all I want,
I have finished)

90 "Or steal through a garden" means
(I move very quietly, I take the garden, I make a lot of noise)

91 "Rave and riot" means
(lift up things, do a lot of damage, stamp on things)

92 "Carry a house-top" means
(lift up the house, can move the house, do damage to the roof)

93–100 Add each word to a suffix or prefix to make the opposite.
thought   own   like   power   please   help   hope   credit

dis .... less

dis .... less

dis .... less

dis .... less

26

Underline the right answers.

I don't like the look of little Fan, mother,
I don't like her looks a little bit.
Her face — well, it's not exactly different,
But there's something wrong with it.
She went down to the sea-shore yesterday,
And she talked to somebody there,
Now she won't do anything but sit
And comb out her yellow hair.
Her eyes are shiny and she sings, mother,
Like nobody ever sang before.
Perhaps they gave her something queer to eat,
Down by the rocks on the shore.
Speak to me, speak, little Fan dear,
Aren't you feeling very well?
Where have you been and what are you singing,
And what's that seaweedy smell?
Where did you get that shiny comb, love
And those pretty coral beads so red?
Yesterday you had two legs, I'm certain
But now there's something else instead.
I don't like the look of little Fan, mother,
You'd best go and close the door.
Quick now, or she'll be gone for ever
On the rocks by the brown sandy shore.

Little Fan by James Reeves

1 The writer first notices that Fan's (hair, looks, face, singing) is
   different.

2 Yesterday Fan had (been ill, gone to the shore, eaten something bad)

3 Today all Fan does is (talk, swim in the sea, comb her hair)

4 The word "speak" is used twice in line 13. Why?
   (It shows the writer is worried, Fan is not listening, Fan doesn't hear)

5–6 What two new things has she? (Shiny comb, coral beads, yellow hair)

7   What do you think has happened to her legs?
     (She has hurt them, they have turned into a tail, she can't walk)

8   "Singing like nobody ever sang before" means
     (she did not sing well, she sang sadly, she sang beautifully)

9   The writer tells Fan to (sit down, speak, get well, watch)

10   "Fan's eyes are shiny" means (she is happy, she is tearful,
     she is cross, she is wet)

11–12 What do you think has happened to Fan? (She is in love, she has been
     captured by someone evil, she has become a mermaid, she is very ill)

13   The mother is told to (make Fan well, make Fan talk, keep an eye on her

14   The writer is afraid that Fan will (die, close the door, disappear)

Complete the following words.

15   ..... oa ..... Resembles a frog   16   .....oa ..... A young horse

17   ..... oa ..... Something that is lent   18   .....oa ..... To wet, to soften

19   ..... oa ..... Related to a sheep   20   ..... oa ..... An outer garment

21   ..... oa ..... A small vessel for travelling on water

22   ..... oa ..... To wander

Complete the following:

23   Black is to white as private is to ....

24   Quiet is to noisy as sweet is to ....

25   Go is to come as exit is to ....

26   Good is to bad as praise is to ....

27   Young is to old as child is to ....

28   Hard is to soft as mean is to ....

One word in each line does not rhyme with the other words. Underline it.

29   tough   cough   gruff   puff   rough   fluff

30   bowl   mole   dole   coal   fowl   soul

31   suite   heat   peat   mate   meet   neat

32   gear   pear   bare   fair   dare   hair

28

33	rear	near	dear	fear	bear	hear
34	draught	drought	laughed	craft	daft	raft

Form nouns from the verbs on the left.

35 begin   The .... of the book was not very exciting.

36 invent   His .... has proved very useful.

37 laugh   The .... of the crowd could be heard from outside.

38 weigh   She had put on a lot of ....

39 solve   Tom found the .... to the problem.

40 speak   Before he presented the prizes, the Chairman made an interesting ....

Write a word in each space so that the second pair of words agree in the same way as the first pair.

41 friend/enemy   harmony/........................

42 owl/hoots   horse/........................

43 cat/feline   dog/........................

44 husband/wife   actor/........................

45 speck/dirt   drop/........................

46 book/booklet   hill/........................

47 infant/infantile   crime/........................

48 country/rural   town/........................

49–52   Four words have been left out of the poem below. Can you work out what they are? Remember that line 2 rhymes with line 4.

The king walked in his garden green
Where grew a marvellous ....
And out of its leaves came singing birds,
By one, and two, and ....
The first bird had wings of white,
The second had wings of ....
The .... had wings of deepest blue
Most beauteous to behold

Write a one-word definition of each of the following words.

53 unimpeded .... **54** dejected ....

55 courteous .... **56** spectators ....

57 desisted .... **58** endeavour ....

Form nouns from the words on the left to complete the following sentences.

59 prepare   Their work was not very good because they had not done enough ....

60 lose   The .... of her money upset Mrs. Walker very much.

61 resemble   The .... between mother and daughter was remarkable.

On the left of the page is a list of verbs, and on the right a list of adverbs. In the space, write the number of the adverb which best describes the verb.

62 listened   ( )   **63** wandered   ( )   (1) promptly
(2) bitterly
64 answered   ( )   **65** helped   ( )   (3) politely
(4) impartially
66 requested   ( )   **67** began   ( )   (5) intently
(6) thoughtfully
68 sobbed   ( )   **69** judge   ( )   (7) aimlessly
(8) willingly

Write the correct number in each space.

70 A person who designs buildings   ( )   (1) optician

71 A person who studies the stars   ( )   (2) plumber

72 A person who makes spectacles   ( )   (3) dictator

73 A person who performs operations   ( )   (4) astronomer

74 A person who mends pipes and taps   ( )   (5) architect

75 A person who is a despot, a tyrant   ( )   (6) surgeon

76 Write one word which has the same meaning as "the line where sea and sky seem to meet". ....

77 Write one word which has the same meaning as "the air around us". ....

78 Write one word which has the same meaning as "to slide smoothly and easily". ....

79–82 The letter below was written by Harry Canavali, who lives at 23, High Street, Beverley, to John Minor at WWH Products, of Sealand Road Trading Estate, Chester, on December 1st 1993. Complete the letter by writing their names and addresses and the date in the correct places.

....

....

....

....

....

....

....

    Thank you for your letter. I am glad to know that Miss Bell, from the Science Department, will be able to visit us next month. Thank you for making the arrangements.

                 Yours faithfully,

....

Complete the following table.

	male	female	young
91–92	bull	....	....
93–94	....	lioness	....
95–96	....	....	piglet
97–98	stag	....	....
99–100	....	duck	....

Underline the right answers.

The church door was shut and there was never a glimmer of candle-light although it was nearly dark with the pouring rain. I walked slowly, dragging back, yet constrained to move forward as the music came in elvish sweetness. Mrs. Pluck never played like that; her music was faltering and broken except when she thumped out a well-known hymn. This was no hymn, it wasn't sacred music at all, and for that I was glad, but it was unearthly and fairy, as if the wind had come down to earth to play a harp of willow boughs. It was unlike anything I had ever heard, and I stood in the church porch sheltering from the rain, listening, hesitating. I felt dizzy and sick and I began to tremble. I unlatched the great door and slowly pushed it open. The church was in pitch darkness as if it were the middle of the night. The blackness lightened and I could distinguish a figure crouched by the font. It was Arabella with a small harp in her hands.

From *A Traveller in Time* by Alison Uttley

1 "There was never a glimmer" means (they never lit the church, there was a small light, there was no light)

2 Was it night time? (Yes, no, we are not told)

3 "Dragging back" means (I didn't want to go forward, I was being dragged back, someone was holding me)

4 "Constrained to move forward" means (something stopped me going on, something stopped me going back, I was compelled to go on)

5 Mrs. Pluck was (a school teacher, the church organist, someone visiting the church)

6–7 Her playing was (good, full of mistakes, even, hesitant)

8 I was glad that (I was in church, it wasn't Mrs. Pluck who was playing, it wasn't church music)

9 The music resembled (fairy music, great music, church music)

10 How do you play a harp? (With a bow, with your hands, you blow into it)

11 I felt sick and dizzy because (I was ill, I was cold, I was frightened, I was a child)

Write one word which has the same meaning as the words in heavy type.

12 The bread is **not fresh**. ....

13 They went on holiday **each year**. ....

14 Sue goes there quite **often**. ....

15 She **was sorry** that she had been naughty. ....

16 Tom **made up his mind** to go to the cinema. ....

17 The **people who had been watching** clapped loudly when the play ended. ....

18 The **people at the church service** listened attentively to the vicar's sermon. ....

Complete the following sentences.

19 Clocks made in Switzerland are .... clocks.

20 Dates grown in Turkey are .... dates.

21 Bacon from Denmark is .... bacon.

22 Olives grown in Greece are .... olives.

23 Bulbs grown in Holland are .... bulbs.

Change the word on the left to the past tense.

24 catch   I .... the last bus home.

25 lie   I .... in bed reading for about an hour.

26 fight   The boys .... against the gang from High Street.

27 go   We .... to London every Easter.

28 hide   They .... in the cupboard under the stairs.

Write the plural of the following words.

    29 domino ....   **30** chimney ....

    31 country ....   **32** fox ....

Complete the words in the following sentences.

    33 She made a list of the stat............. they needed.

    34 It wasn't moving at all; it was quite stat............... .

    35 The pro........... preached to the people.

    36 The business made a substantial pro........... last year.

    37 Felicity enjoyed watching the ....er........... on television.

    38 Alan always had ....er........... for his breakfast.

Underline the subject of each sentence, and put a ring round the object.

39–40   The naughty boy upset his teacher.

41–42   Give the pen to me.

43–44   In Britain people drive on the left-hand side of the road.

45–46   When playing the piano Sean sits on a stool.

Complete the words:

    47 The girl was very sad. She was un ....

    48 The road was bumpy. It was un ....

    49 The plum was not ready for eating. It was un ....

    50 He had taken off his clothes. He had un ....

    51 They did not know what to do. They were un ....

    52 People didn't like him. He was un ....

Form adjectives from the words on the left.

53   sense   She gave a .... reply.

54   triangle   It was a .... piece.

55   study   He is a .... boy.

56   energy   It was an .... dance.

57   comic   He pulled a .... face.

58   angel   It was an .... sound.

Complete the following:

59   A sett is the home of a ....

60   A dovecote is the home of a ....

61   An .... lives in an eyrie.

62   A lodge is the home of a ....

63   A .... lives in a drey.

64   An earth is the home of a ....

Underline the word which is the same part of speech as the word on the left.

65   **easily**   dull   well   effective   slow   love

66   **size**   big   gigantic   enormous   brakes   fill

67   **affable**   bitter   affair   affably   awake   was

68   **them**   groups   but   friends   me   teacher

Write the word which is the past tense of the word on the left.

69   buy   Mum .... the Christmas presents early this year.

70   hang   We .... up the decorations and decorated the tree.

71   shrink   When I washed my sweater it ....

72   grind   I love the smell of coffee which has just been ....

73   blow   The toddler .... bubbles with his new pipe.

74   creep   They made her jump as they .... up behind her.

75   sell   We .... all the tickets for our concert.

Give the opposites of the following words by using prefixes.

76 advantage .... 77 considerate ....

78 fallible .... 79 perfect ....

80–88 Punctuate this sentence.

i will never believe it though replied the old lady never

....

Write a shorter word to define each of the long words below.

89 conflagration .... 90 interior ....

91 genuine .... 92 proprietor ....

93 distinguished .... 94 courageous ....

Complete each line by forming a noun from the word on the left.

95 deliver The .... of the mail is erratic on the island.

96 cancel The .... of the order caused considerable trouble.

97 deceive Mr. Jones was very upset. He said that her .... was hard to forgive.

98 injure Fortunately the .... was not serious.

99 succeed Angus was delighted at his .... in the competition.

100 conclude The story reached an interesting ....

36

Underline the right answers.

Gus is the Cat at the Theatre Door.
His name, as I ought to have told you before,
Is really Asparagus. That's such a fuss
To pronounce, that we usually call him just Gus.
His coat's very shabby, he's thin as a rake,
And he suffers from palsy that makes his paw shake.
Yet he was, in his youth, quite the smartest of Cats—
But no longer a terror to mice and to rats.
For he isn't the Cat that he was in his prime;
Though his name was quite famous, he says, in its time.
And whenever he joins his friends at their club
(Which takes place at the back of the neighbouring pub)
He loves to regale them, if someone else pays,
With anecdotes drawn from his palmiest days.

For he once was a Star of the highest degree—
He has acted with Irving, he's acted with Tree,
And he likes to relate his success on the Halls,
Where the Gallery once gave him seven cat-calls.
But his grandest creation, as he loves to tell,
Was Firefrorefiddle, the Fiend of the Fell.

"I have played," so he says, "every possible part,
And I used to know seventy speeches by heart.
I'd extemporise back-chat, I knew how to gag,
And I knew how to let the cat out of the bag.
I knew how to act with my back and my tail;
With an hour of rehearsal, I never could fail.
I'd a voice that would soften the hardest of hearts,
Whether I took the lead, or in character parts.
I have sat by the bedside of poor Little Nell;
When the Curfew was rung, then I swung on the bell.
In the Pantomime season I never fell flat,
And once I understudied Dick Whittington's Cat.
But my grandest creation, as history will tell,
Was Firefrorefiddle, the Fiend of the Fell."

From *Gus the Theatre Cat* by T. S. Eliot

1 "Extemporise" means (to prepare a speech, to copy, to extend,
   to speak without preparation, to talk rudely)

2 In the poem a "gag" is (a king of bag, a joke, a cloth stuffed into someone's mouth, laughter)

3–4 Name the two actors mentioned. (Irving, Tree, Little Nell, Dick Whittington)

5 What was the most important part Gus had played? (Little Nell, Firefrorefiddle, Dick Whittington's Cat)

6 "The Halls" are (Music Halls, Parish Halls, halls in houses)

7 A part of the theatre is mentioned; it is (the Gallery, the Curfew, the Halls)

8 "Every possible part" means (parts which were suitable for him, all the parts he had been offered, all kinds of parts)

9 "Back-chat" is (reversing words, cheeky answers, having a chat at the back)

10 "To let the cat out of the bag" means (to play Dick Whittington, to disclose a secret, to be always quarrelling)

11 "Taking the lead" means (playing the leading part, being in charge of the animals, pretending to be the chief)

12 Gus met his friends (in a club, in a theatre, behind a pub)

13 Gus received cat-calls at the end of his act. If successful an actor would receive (cat-calls, curtain calls, roll calls)

14 Name the illness he was suffering from. ....

15 He "never fell flat" means (he never tumbled, people liked him, he wasn't an acrobat)

These words have been left out of this poem. Can you fill them in?

battle　　　rain　　　ditches　　　plain　　　cattle　　　witches

16 Faster than fairies, faster than ....

17 Bridges and houses, hedges and ....

18 And charging along like troops in a ....

19 All through the meadows the horses and ....

20 All of the sights of the hill and the ....

21 Fly as fast as driving ....

Put the correct word in each space.

referee   dentist   chef   steeplejack   blacksmith
decorator   orphan   chemist

22 An expert male cook is a ....

23 A person who repairs high buildings is a ....

24 A person who paints and papers walls is a ....

25 A person who makes up medicines is a ....

26 A person who looks after our teeth is a ....

27 A child whose parents are dead is an ....

28 A person who makes sure footballers keep to the rules ia a ....

29 A person who shoes horses is a ....

The list below contains words of similar meaning to those on the left.
Can you pair them?

absurd   attempt   mould   surprise   doubt   keep   complete

30 astonish ....

31 retain ....

32 finish ....

33 shape ....

34 ridiculous ....

35 try ....

36 uncertainty ....

In each space write the correct preposition.

37 I am beginning to despair .... Jane ever doing better work.

38 That cake is similar .... one that Dad makes.

39 Mr. Bell was very angry .... Tom when he broke the window.

40 Miss Jones said that she did not approve .... the way I did my hair.

41 David said that he did not like being accused .... being unkind.

42 The prize money is being divided .... Jonathan and his brother.

43 Mum said that she could rely .... me to do the shopping.

Write a conjunction to join the two parts of each sentence.

44 The sun was warm .... it was December.

45 I will wait .... you have finished.

46 You don't have to do it .... you want to.

47 He did not know .... to go for a swim or play cricket.

48 She was sent home .... she was not well.

49 I want to go to Italy .... I can afford it.

50–53 We are interrupting our programmes to give you an urgent police message. About 10 a.m. today some dangerous drugs were stolen from a doctor's blue Cortina car which was parked in High Street, Lowby. The drugs look like pink sweets, and we are told that they could be very dangerous, particularly if swallowed by children. Anyone who can help the police please telephone Lowby 123456 as soon as possible.

Underline the statements which are true.

This notice appeared in a newspaper.
The doctor's car was parked in High Street this morning.
The drugs are not dangerous if taken by adults.
The drugs look like sweets.
This announcement was made on television or radio—or both.
The police want to interview the doctor.
The police are in a hurry as the doctor shouldn't have been in High Street.
It is urgent because people may have swallowed the drugs.

Insert the necessary quotation marks, and underline the words which should then start with capital letters.

54 The girls heard a lot of noise, and someone shouted, where is the door?

55 The teacher put down the chalk, and shouted, hasn't anyone finished yet?

56 Dennis, who was much younger, cried, when will we get home?

57 The shopkeeper said crossly, leave those toys alone.

Write one word instead of the words in heavy type.

58 When she was washing up Jane broke the cup **by accident.** ....

59 The boy spoke to his teacher **with respect.** ....

60 Darren threw down the pen **in anger.** ....

61 Lisa drew the picture **with skill.** ....

62 Timothy chased the burglar **without fear.** ....

63 Moyra walked up on to the platform **with pride.** ....

Use words ending in **ant** or **ent** to complete the following sentences.

64 The girl does not know much about painting. She is ig.............. about it.

65 They did as they were told. They were ob..............

66 The children looked around carefully. They were ob..............

67 Julia was very lazy. She was in..............

68 We had lots of apples on our tree. The crop was ab..............

69 The boy had not committed the crime. He was in..............

70 I could see through the glass. It was trans..............

Pair off the following, and then write the correct number in the space.

71 He broke his lace .....( )....   (1) when we touched it

72 We woke her up .....( )....   (2) until they sang it better

73 The class practised the song .....( )....   (3) because she was very tired

74 The boys will be cold .....( )....   (4) before he goes to bed

75 She went to bed .....( )....   (5) while he was tying up his shoes

76 She must hurry up .....( )....   (6) unless they run about

77 He must clean his teeth .....( )....   (7) though we went in quietly

78 The ice cracked .....( )....   (8) if she wants to be early

41

Write the superlative form of the adjective on the left.

79 clever That is the .... answer of all.

80 poor   The .... families live there.

81 bad   They reported the .... gale for ten years.

82 ugly   She was the .... of the sisters.

83 red   My apple is the .... I have ever seen.

84 generous Mum is the .... person I know.

Write these in the possessive case.
Example: The bone of the dog. The dog's bone

85 The hats of the girls   ....

86 The sting of a wasp   ....

87 The home of Tess   ....

88 The books of the children ....

89 The bike of his friend   ....

90 The mane of the lion   ....

Complete the following proverbs.

91 When the cat's away the .... will play.

92 One man's .... is another man's poison.

93 Fair .... is no robbery.

94 Don't put all your .... in one basket.

95 Every .... has his day.

In each line one word is incorrect. Underline that word, and then, in the space, write what the word should be.

96 Which of the two is the best?   ....

97 The house were all they had.   ....

98 Neither Jack or Jill can go up the hill. ....

99 Ian and me are going to the party.   ....

100 Dad gave the apples to Gary and I.   ....

Underline the right answers.

We had to be ready to put him to bed at six o'clock sharp, and if we were late he would stalk furiously up and down outside his drawer, his fur standing on end with rage. We had to learn not to slam doors shut without first looking to see if Pavlo was sitting on top, because, for some reason, he liked to sit on doors and meditate. But our worst crime, according to him, was when we went out and left him for an afternoon. When we returned he would leave us in no doubt as to his feelings on the subject; we would be in disgrace. He would turn his back on us in disgust when we tried to talk to him; he would go and sit in a corner and glower at us, his little face screwed up into a scowl. After half an hour or so he would, very reluctantly, forgive us and with regal condescension accept a lump of sugar and some warm milk before retiring to bed. The marmoset's moods were most human, for he would scowl and mutter at you when he felt bad tempered, and, very probably, try to give you a nip. When he was feeling affectionate, however, he would approach you with a loving expression on his face, poking his tongue out and in rapidly, and smacking his lips, climb on to your shoulder and give your ear a series of passionate nibbles.

From *Portrait of Pavlo* by Gerald Durrell

1 Pavlo was a (human being, dog, marmoset, monkey)

2 Pavlo slept in a (bed, drawer, nest, corner)

3 To "stalk" is to (sway, saunter, swing, walk stiffly and proudly, balance)

4 "Six o'clock sharp" means (just before six, just after six, about six, at six o'clock exactly)

5 To "meditate" is to (sleep, mediate, think, shout)

6 What did Pavlo most dislike? (Being left alone, being put to bed, someone slamming doors)

7 "Reluctantly" means (recently, regally, unwillingly, pleasantly)

8 To "glower" is to (glow, throw things at us, glare)

9 For how long did Pavlo's moods last?
(For half an hour, until six o'clock, for about half an hour, for hours)

10 Pavlo put out his tongue when (he was pleased, he was being rude, he was cross, he wanted food)

11 When Pavlo was pleased he had a loving expression. Which one word in the passage has an opposite meaning? (Scowl, condescension, nibbles)

12 (Human, regal, affectionate, passionate) means "like a king".

13-16 One word in each column is spelled wrongly. Underline that word.

villain	sylabus	trousers	tragedy
quay	bicycle	yolk	debt
opponent	career	stalk	pavillion
apostle	suite	decieve	earnest
honorary	favour	advise	enough
seperate	campaign	operator	height

In each space fill in the correct colour.

17 The pages of the manuscript were .... with age.

18 The old man stamped his foot, and his face turned .... with rage.

19 When Martin finished the job his hands were as .... as coal.

20 After building a snowman, the boy's hands were .... with cold.

21 The owl screeched, and the girl's face turned .... with fright.

Form nouns from the words on the left to complete the sentences.

22 provide   The .... of food was her responsibility.

23 confuse   After the raid the .... was terrible to see.

24 punctual   Her .... was noticed by the teacher.

44

25 do   Tim's brave .... was mentioned in the paper.

26 coward   Yellow is often associated with ....

27 commence   The .... of the play was greeted with cheers.

28 deep   There was not enough .... of water for diving.

Two words are often combined to form one longer word. Pair off the words below, and write the correct number in each space.

29 stone ....   30 knee ....   (1) head   (5) shoe
                                                 (2) deep   (6) arms
31 fire ....   32 horse ....   (3) mail   (7) work
                                                 (4) roads
33 black ....   34 cross ....

35 fore ....

Underline the word in each line which has a different meaning from the others.

36 promise   peace   pledge   vow   oath

37 aid   assist   support   help   oppose

38 joke   blunder   oversight   fault   error

39 attack   charge   cost   assault   aggression

40 multiply   divide   enlarge   increase   extend

41 renovate   renew   regenerate   remove   revive

42 jeer   deride   rebel   mock   ridicule

In each space, write the number of the most suitable adverb.

(1) longingly (2) heroically (3) patiently (4) attentively (5) feverishly (6) thoroughly (7) spitefully

43 The whole class listened .... to their teacher.

44 A good workman does a job ....

45 To repeat gossip is to talk ....

46 The children looked .... at the presents on the tree.

47 After the crash the rescuers worked ....

48 The invalid waited .... for the doctor to visit her.

49 The men who were trapped dug .... through the rubble.

Write the past participle of each of these verbs.

Example: sing sung

50 begin ....

51 ring ....

52 drink ....

53 write ....

54 steal ....

55 find ....

Complete the following:

56 Arrival is to departure as ascend is to ....

57 Reward is to punishment as maximum is to ....

58 Describe is to descriptive as extend is to ....

59 Sense is to sensible as humour is to ....

60 Fail is to failure as believe is to ....

61 Grow is to growth as lose is to ....

In each line one word is wrong. Underline that word, and write what it should be in the space.

62 The cinema and the theatre was both open. ....

63 She was the best of the two competitors. ....

64 Dad took the fireworks from Sarah and I. ....

65 Who's book is this? ....

66 The choir sung well. ....

67 Beside playing cricket and swimming she can row. ....

68 I must buy a license for my dog. ....

69 The chimney was struck by lightening. ....

In each space write the adjective formed from the noun on the left.

70 nation   The earthquake was a .... disaster.

71 humour   A .... article appeared in the paper.

72 fame   Lord Nelson was a very .... admiral.

73 energy   Rugger is a very .... game.

74 bible   Naaman was a .... character.

75 mischief   Timmy is a very .... little boy.

Give the plural of:

76 torpedo .... 77 crisis ....

78 sheep .... 79 calf ....

80 valley ....

81–91 Fill in the missing words.

"Is there anybody .... ?" said the Traveller,

Knocking on the moonlit........................;

And his horse .... the silence champed the grasses

.... the forest's ferny floor.

And a bird flew .... out of the turret,

.... the Traveller's head:

And he smote upon the door a .... time;

"Is there .... there?" he said.

........................no-one descended to the Traveller;

No head from the leaf-fringed sill

Leaned over and looked into his grey eyes,

Where he stood perplexed and ....

The Listeners
by
Walter de la Mare

Put the correct word in each space.

eavesdropper   manager   benefactor   proprietor   umpire

92 A person who gives money to benefit others is a ....

93 One who sees that there is fair play is an ....

94 One who listens to conversations he is not meant to hear
is an ....

95 A person who owns something is a ....

96 A person who runs a business is a ....

Write a five-letter word which is the opposite of the word in heavy type.

97 The story was completely **true**. ....

98 The man mumbled a **blessing**. ....

99 The knife is **sharp**. ....

100 The wallpaper was very **ornate**. ....

Underline the right answers.

He had finished. The Dean's watch was now once more repaired and he knew he could not have made a better job of it. He held it open in the palm of his hands and gazed at it with veneration, his jeweller's eyepiece in his eye. It was inscribed "George Graham fecit 1712". At that date Graham had been at the height of his powers. The inscription took Isaac back to the old bow-windowed shop in Fleet Street, next door to the Duke of Marlborough's Head tavern, which had been a place of pilgrimage for him when as a lad he had served his apprenticeship in Clerkenwell. Graham had worked in that shop and lived and died in the humble rooms above it. Charles II's horologist, Thomas Tompion, whom men called the father of English clockmaking, had been Graham's uncle. Both men had been masters of the Clockmakers' Company, and they had been buried in the same tomb in Westminster Abbey. Whenever he held the Dean's watch in his hands Isaac remembered that George Graham's hands had also held it and that perhaps Tompion, in his old age, had looked upon his nephew's handiwork and commended it.

From *The Dean's watch* by Elizabeth Goudge

1 Was the watch mended well? (Yes, no, it could have been better)

2 "Veneration" is (agitation, reverence, interest, curiosity)

3 "Fecit 1712" means (found in 1712, died in 1712, made in 1712)

4 "Bow-windows" are (windows with curtains, circular windows, curved windows, broken windows)

5 Fleet Street is now famous for (clockmakers, taverns, newspapers, tea markets, meat markets)

6 A horologist is (a clockmaker, a gardener, a pilgrim)

7 In which town did these people live and die? (London, Leeds, New York)

8 "At the height of his powers" means (when he had grown as tall as possible, when he was a man, when he was most skilled)

9 Who was the royal clockmaker? (Thomas Tompion, George Graham, Isaac, Charles)

10 "The father of English clockmaking" means (he was the father of the best clockmaker, he was the early leader of English clockmakers, he was the first Englishman to make clocks)

11 An "inscription" is (an inspection, an insertion, an engraving, an endorsement)

12 What is the word used for Isaac's training? (Apprenticeship, veneration, pilgrimage)

13 "Humble" means (modest, humdrum, attic, haunted, small)

14–20 Can you change BOAT to SHIP, and READ to BOOK (by changing one letter at a time) in the spaces given?

BOAT   READ

....

....

....

....   BOOK
SHIP

Turn the following into indirect speech.

21 "Will you please help me, Mike?" asked his mother.

His mother asked Mike ....

22 "Are you going to the baths, Tom?" asked Shaun.

Shaun asked Tom ....

23 "I may go to the cinema," said Matthew.

Matthew said that ....

49

Make longer words by pairing these two lists.

24 tortoise ....   25 dish ....

26 over ....   27 finger ....

28 marks ....   29 loop ....

30 hair ....

brush
power
hole
washer
nail
man
shell

The next day was as gloomy as the day before. The sky was overcast. Peter went about with the same heavy weight on his conscience. He sat down under the same rock and his thoughts turned around in the same circle.

31–34 Underline the statements which are correct.

The weather yesterday had not been good.
Today it was brighter.
Peter was feeling dizzy.
He kept on thinking the same thoughts.
He was very worried.
He was carrying a heavy load.
He was worried yesterday.

Complete the following:

35 The lakes of Italy are called the .... lakes.

36 The steppes of Russia are the .... steppes.

37 Fish from Iceland is .... fish.

38 Hats from Mexico are .... hats.

39 An ice-cream from Naples is a .... ice-cream.

Write one word in place of the words in heavy type.

40 She worked out the answers to the sums **in her head.** ....

41 He always worked **in a steady fashion.** ....

42 Mum waited for Tara **with patience.** ....

43 **Now and then** we go to the theatre. ....

44 John did his work **without thought.** ....

50

The answers to the next set of questions all end in **ify**.

45 To put into a class ....

46 To make larger ....

47 To make beautiful ....

48 To make pure ....

49 To make, or bring, peace ....

In each space write the name of a sound.

50 Sue was glad to be indoors because she could hear
the .... of the rain on the windows.

51 We could hear the .... of the leaves when the wind blew.

52 A loud .... of thunder made them scurry for shelter.

53 The .... of the explosion filled the air with dust.

54 When the hinge .... they knew they should oil it.

In the space write the number of the correct definition.

55 A philatelist is ....( )....   (1) a person who makes maps

56 An antiquary is ....( )....   (2) a person who studies plants

57 A cartographer is ....( )....   (3) a person who studies animals

58 A surveyor is ....( )....   (4) a person who collects stamps

59 A botanist is ....( )....   (5) a person who studies rocks

60 A zoologist is ....( )....   (6) a person who measures land

61 A geologist is ....( )....   (7) a person who collects old things

Give the plural of the following words.

62 life`   ....   63 salmon   ....

64 wharf   ....   65 monkey   ....

66 thief   ....   67 pony   ....

Give the superlative of these adjectives.

68 bad   ....   69 lovely   ....

70 good   ....   71 noisy   ....

In the space write the number of the adverb which best suits the verb.

72 peered ...( )...   (1) audibly

73 spoke ...( )...   (2) studiously

74 worked ...( )...   (3) legibly

75 dressed ...( )...   (4) suspiciously

76 hung ...( )...   (5) perilously

77 wrote ...( )...   (6) smartly

Pair these columns of words to make compound words. Write the number in the space.

78 key ...( )...   (1) tight

79 day ...( )...   (2) light

80 cloud ...( )...   (3) knife

81 water ...( )...   (4) ring

82 pen ...( )...   (5) knob

83 door ...( )...   (6) burst

84–100 Punctuate this.

oh no i think ive lost my purse cried mrs davis id better tell the police

....

....

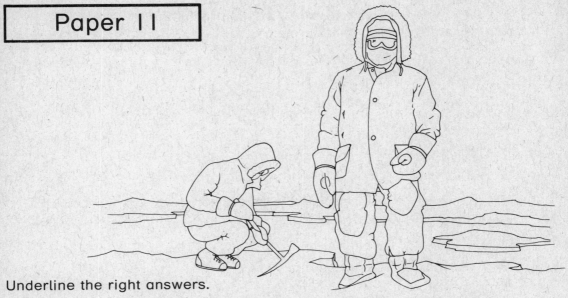

Underline the right answers.

"A man's first mistake in the Arctic is usually his last," says Squadron Leader Scott Alexander of the Royal Canadian Air Force's survival training school at Cambridge Bay, 200 miles above the Arctic Circle. Here, in a land of snow, ice and rock, mauled by vicious polar winds, a handful of experts are teaching Canadian airmen how to stay alive in the event of an emergency landing. More than 2000 students take this course annually. "If you survive, you've passed," the men jest.

The course begins in heavily timbered country in Alberta. Here the 30 or 40 men in a group receive ten days instruction in bush experience. Nothing is overlooked that might help a man live through an emergency. Then comes the most gruelling session. Dressed in heavy survival gear and parachute harness the men fly to Cambridge Bay. Once they have built their snow houses, lit the Primus stoves, and prepared a meal from emergency rations the outlook brightens. Bedtime comes early because dampness increases the danger of freezing. Socks, mitts, flying boots and shirt all go to bed with the man—to be dried during the night by body heat.

1 A man's first mistake is usually his last because
(he learns quickly, a mistake usually causes death, he is only allowed to make one mistake)

2 "Above the Arctic Circle" means (inside the Arctic Circle, flying over the Arctic Circle, south of the Arctic Circle)

3 "Mauled by winds" means (driven by winds, battered by winds, melted by the winds)

4 The students do this course (each year, frequently, usually once)

5 "Heavily timbered" means with (wooden buildings, buildings with rafters, dense forest, a camp of wooden huts)

6 "The outlook brightens" means (men feel more cheerful, the weather improves, the sun comes out)

7 Their clothes are dried by (Primus stove, wearing them in bed, hanging them up)

8 To "jest" is to (guess, state, curse, joke, prophesy)

9 "Bush" is (wild country, forest land, cultivated land)

10 It is a very tough course. Apart from the first sentence what other remark tells you this? (If you survive you've passed, bedtime comes early, handful of experts)

11 A gruelling session is (when they learn to cook, doing something they find extremely hard, an emergency landing)

12 From which country are the airmen? (Alberta, Cambridge, America, Canada)

Complete the following words, which fit the definitions on the right-hand side.

13 .... ea ....   to walk, to step on

14 .... ea ....   water vapour

15 .... ea ....   noise made by sheep

16 .... ea ....   fatty part of milk from which butter is made

Underline the word which is the same part of speech as the word on the left.

17 **solve**   solution   exam   boy   do   and

18 **tidal**   sea   harbour   it   boatman   fishy

19 **seat**   it   shade   sit   tired   after

20 **about**   shout   fair   bout   after   laugh

21 **woollen**   furious   Wales   sock   country   jumper

22 **tell**   story   why   yesterday   shelve   chapter

Complete the following:

23 Cat is to mouse as spider is to ....

24 Tuesday is to Thursday as March is to ....

25 Bird is to wing as fish is to ....

26 Collar is to neck as cuff is to ....

Below are some words, and, on the right of the page, a list of their meanings. Pair them off, and write the correct number in the space.

27 diagram ....( )....

28 dialect ....( )....

29 dialogue ....( )....

30 diameter ....( )....

31 diagonal ....( )....

32 diamond ....( )....

(1) a straight line joining angles of a figure which are not adjacent

(2) an illustration to explain a point

(3) a variety of language peculiar to a certain district

(4) a valuable gem

(5) a straight line drawn through the centre of a circle from circumference to circumference

(6) a conversation between two or more people

Underline the correct word in the brackets.

33 They announced the (berth, birth) of the royal baby.

34 She slept in the lower (berth, birth).

35 I made a black-(currant, current) tart today.

36 The man got a shock from the electric (currant, current).

37 The (miner, minor) went down the pit shaft.

38 A (miner, minor) is a person under eighteen years of age.

39 A (purl, pearl) is found in an oyster.

40 (Purl, pearl) is a stitch used in knitting.

Underline the prepositions in the following lines.

41 They threw the ball across the playground.

42 Maria sat beside her friend Caroline.

43 They could not see beyond the hills.

44 Steven threw the ball and it went through the window.

45 Underneath the desk they found the rubber.

46 "Put the book on the table," Mum said.

Underline the verbs in these sentences.

47–48   Julie wondered what she should wear to the party.

49–50   I am buying a new car from the garage where my friend works.

51   Stop, thief!

Complete the following similes.

52   As .... as a bat   53   As .... as pie

54   As .... as a cricket   55   As .... as leather

56   As .... as dust   57   As .... as a fiddle

58   As .... as a judge   59   As .... as a mouse

Use a form of the word on the left to answer each clue.

60   compliment   Given as a compliment   ....

61   person   Belonging to a person   ....

62   anger   Those who show anger are   ....

63   courage   Those who show courage are   ....

64   deceit   Those who are not straightforward
                   are   ....

65   luxury   Full of luxury   ....

Use these words to fill in the spaces below.

party   flight   series   litter   group   bunch

66   A .... of islands   67   A .... of puppies

68   A .... of programmes   69   A .... of bananas

70   A .... of friends   71   A .... of stairs

Write these words in the plural.

72   roof   73   axe   ....

74   flute   75   shelf ....

76   half   77   piano ....

56

78 A person from Sweden is called a ....

79 A person from Poland is called a ....

80 A person from Germany is called a ....

81 A person from the West Indies is called a ....

82 A person from China is called a ....

83 A person from Scotland is called a ....

84–88 Fill in the missing words.

We arrived at the .... in good time. First we checked in our luggage; my sister thought her case was too .... but it was .... right. We then went to buy presents in the duty- .... shop. Soon our flight was called. We boarded the plane, fastened our seat .... and were off.

Here is a table which compares adjectives. Can you fill in the spaces?

Example:	good	better	best
89–90	little	....	....
91–92	....	....	most
93–94	....	finer	....

Give a one-word definition of the following words.

95 fatigued ....

96 deficiency ....

97 precarious ....

98 renovate ....

99 pedestrian ....

100 submerge ....

Underline the right answers.

Sabotage is an essential part of espionage. The spy must know a great deal about demolition charges and booby traps. And he must be able to fit such things in the dark.

He is trained in the art of burglary, using simple tools or, better still, improvisation. He must be adept in fashioning and using skeleton keys and pick-locks.

He must not only know the tools of his trade; he must be able to teach their use to others. Some spies operate single-handed, others are part of an organisation. The leader of the group must be able to brief his subordinates – who may be untrained local people.

He must be expert at unarmed combat. A shot attracts attention – the spy must be trained to kill silently.

He is even taught some details of disguise; not wigs and whiskers, which are rather too obvious, but small changes which could deceive an observer. He could appear to be about two inches shorter by practising a slouch. He can alter the shape of his face temporarily by stuffing slices of apple or potato under his cheeks. There are solutions which will darken his skin or bleach it. The dyeing of his hair will effect a considerable change in his appearance.

From *Spy school* by Bernard Newman

1 "Sabotage" is (deliberate destruction, sacrilege, accidental damage, a hidden danger)

2 "A subordinate" is (a fellow worker, someone in charge, someone lower in rank)

3 "Improvisation" is (using a complicated machine, using anything which is handy, having improved tools)

4 "Adept" means (accustomed, skilled, keen, not afraid)

5–8 In which ways do they disguise themselves? (Wearing wigs, slouching, wearing false heels, stuffing out their cheeks, wearing false moustaches, changing the colour of their skin, blacking their teeth, dyeing their hair)

9 In this passage the word "charge" means (the cost of something, a package of explosive, having the care of equipment)

10 To brief is to (give instructions, give a short talk, act as a lawyer)

11 A spy usually kills by (shooting, blowing up, strangling)

12 Why must he be able to work in the dark? (Spies don't carry torches, they only work at night, he mustn't be seen)

Fill in the missing letters.

13 Mother Hubbard found no food in the cup .... d.

14 All the children liked chocolate bi .... s.

15 The air around us is called the a .... e.

16 The doctor told me to take my m .... e twice a day.

17 We like birds, and we have a bu .... r that we keep in a cage.

18 The saucepans are made of a .... m.

19 Something old is called an a .... e.

Complete the following by putting in the name of a person.

Example: donate donor

20 advise ....

21 electrify ....

22 save ....

23 pacify ....

24 conquer ....

Turn the following into direct speech.

25 Dad told Gary that he would give him the money on Saturday.

Dad said, ...

26 The teacher warned Jackie to be careful with her writing.

.... warned the teacher.

27 Sandra said that she wanted to get it right that time.

Sandra said, ...

28 Mum told Nicola that she thought she would be able to finish her dress.

Mum said to Nicola, ...

29 Dad told Andrew that he didn't want his help that day.

Dad said to Andrew, ...

In each space write the part of speech of the word in heavy type.

30 Mum is playing a **round** of golf this morning.   ....

31 I had it when I came **round** to see you.   ....

32 The biscuits are in the **round** tin.   ....

33 The boy said that he would **round** up the sheep.   ....

Underline the correct meaning of the following idioms.

34 The game is not worth the candle
(It is a cheap game, something you do is not worth the effort you are putting into it, you would play better if the light were brighter)

35 To fall on one's feet
(To be lucky, to hurt yourself when you jump, to be athletic)

36 To pay through the nose
(To have to put up with a nasty smell, to pay too high a price, to give goods instead of money)

37 To make a mountain out of a mole-hill
(To move land from one place to another, to make a big fuss about a small matter, to make things seem less important than they really are)

Here are sets of adjectives which might be used to describe parts of people's bodies. Which parts are they?

38 straight, white, discoloured, decayed, false ....

39 brown, blue, grey, sparkling, clear ....

40 spotty, tanned, pale, freckled, red ....

41 straight, curly, coarse, fine, silky ....

42 full, thin, sulky, red ....

Complete the following:

43 Hand is to finger as foot is to ....

44 Spain is to Spaniard as Malta is to ....

45 Add is to subtract as compulsory is to ....

46 Give is to take as certainty is to ....

47 Beginning is to end as success is to ....

Write one word instead of the words in heavy type.

48 We **kept out of the way of** Mum because she was cross. ....

49 Mr. Martin said that my work is **getting much better**. ....

50 In case we forgot, we said the message **over and over again**. ....

51 The fraction had to be **turned upside down**. ....

52 **A short time ago** we went to the circus. ....

53 The boy was told to **come back** tomorrow. ....

54 The cyclist knocked over a **person who was walking**. ....

Give the full meaning of the following abbreviations.

55 p.a. .... 56 p & p ....

57 D.I.Y. .... 58 c/o ....

59 Ind. Est. .... 60 Bros. ....

Complete the following:

61 Lace from Belgium is .... lace.

62 Sardines from Portugal are .... sardines.

63 People from Cyprus are ....

64 Towns in Finland are .... towns.

65 Cats from the Isle of Man are .... cats.

66 A gondola in Venice is a .... gondola.

Underline the subject, and put a ring round the object in the following sentences:

67–68 On the stage Marcia wore her long evening dress.

69–70 We are all going on an outing today.

71–72 Because he wanted to look smart, Sean wore his best trousers.

73–74 Diana, who likes housework, cleaned the bath.

Complete the sentences below by using one of these words.

   lonely   barren   bleak   deserted   desolate

75 The house was dark and chilly. There were no curtains at the windows, and the furniture was plain and bare. The atmosphere was very ....

76 When her husband was killed in a car crash the woman could not be comforted, and was quite .... with grief.

77 The girl always played by herself but she did not seem to be ....

78 Part of North America is .... and only small stunted trees grow there.

79 When the soldiers entered the fort they found it had been .... by the enemy.

80-87 Can you fill in the missing words in this poem?

The lion ...., the tiger growls,

Their mouths are open ....,

Then, suddenly, they .... them closed

To trap their .... inside.

They chew their food with strong, white ....

Which sparkle when .... smile.

They lick their .... with long pink ....,

Then yawn and sleep awhile.

Use the words listed below to complete the sentences.

crow   weight   ropes   tether   grindstone

88 The boy knew the .... and finished the job quickly.

89 Jane had been working all day. "I'm at the end of my ....," she said.

90 "How far is it to London?" asked James.
"As the .... flies it is about thirty kilometres."

91 Diana was determined to pass her exam so she kept her nose to the
....

92 If we all pull our .... the show is sure to be a success.

Below are eight pairs of words. Some have opposite meanings and some are similar. Put them in the right columns.

93-100 fresh/stale   spectator/onlooker   system/method   irritate/soothe
fiction/fact   squander/waste   meet/avoid   banish/expel

similar	opposite
....	....
....	....
....	....
....	....

Date

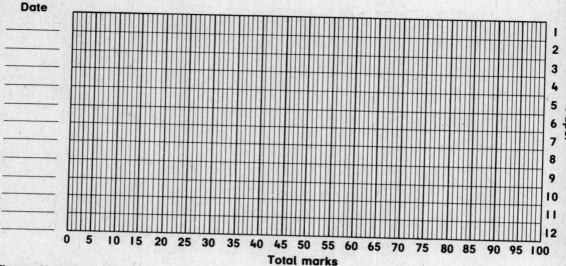

Paper

1
2
3
4
5
6
7
8
9
10
11
12

0 5 10 15 20 25 30 35 40 45 50 55 60 65 70 75 80 85 90 95 100

Total marks

Thomas Nelson and Sons Ltd
Nelson House Mayfield Road
Walton-on-Thames Surrey
KT12 5PL UK

© **J M Bond 1977, 1983, 1986, 1994**

First published by Thomas Nelson and Sons Ltd 1977
Revised edition 1983
Revised edition 1986
This fully revised edition 1994

I(T)P Thomas Nelson is an International
Thomson Publishing Company

I(T)P is used under licence

Pupil's book   ISBN 0-17-424527-0
NPN 9 8 7 6 5
Answer book ISBN 0-17-424528-9
NPN 9 8 7 6 5 4 3

By the same author
First, Second, Third, Fourth and Further Fourth Year
Assessment Papers in Mathematics

First, Second, Third, Fourth and Further Fourth Year
Assessment Papers in English

First, Second, Third, Fourth and Further Fourth
Year Assessment Papers in Reasoning

Printed in Croatia

Poems and extracts reproduced by kind
permission of

Dobson Books Ltd: **Fog in November**
from *Four Seasons* by Leonard Clark (Paper 1)
Faber & Faber Ltd: Extract from **Gus the Theatre
Cat** from *Old Possum's book of Practical Cats*
by T S Eliot (Paper 8)
William Heinemann Ltd: **Little Fan** (Paper 6) and
The Wind (Paper 5) from *The Wandering moon*
by James Reeves
The Literary Trustees of Walter de la Mare and
the Society of Authors as their representative:
Extract from *The Listeners* (Paper 9)
Collins Publishers: Extract from *Portrait of Pavlo*
by Gerald Durrell (Paper 9)
Faber & Faber Ltd: Extract from *A Traveller in
Time* by Alison Uttley (Paper 7)
George Allen & Unwin: Extract from *The Hobbit*
by J R R Tolkien (Paper 6)
Robert Hale Ltd: Extract from *Spy School* by
Bernard Newman (Paper 12)
Hodder & Stoughton Ltd: Extracts from
The Dean's Watch (Paper 10) and *A crock of Gold*
(Paper 2) by Elizabeth Goudge
Penguin Books Ltd: Extract from
Talking to Animals (p37) by Barbara Woodhouse
© Barbara Woodhouse 1970, 1980 (Paper 4)

The publishers have made every attempt to trace
copyright holders of reprinted material, and
apologise for any errors or omissions.